The
Art Of
Escape

Poetry by
Trier Ward

Illustrations by Tarynn Di'Nnovati

Publication Acknowledgements

"Good Years" first appeared in Mad Swirl
(April 10, 2015).

"Among the Rushes" first appeared in Boundless: The Rio
Grande Valley International Poetry Festival
Anthology 2024.

"Bad Girlfriend", "Heavenly Body" and "To a Fighter" first
appeared in Alien Buddha Press (April 2024, ABZ61 Edition).

"Organ Donor', "Rides" and "Waking" first appeared in The
Stygian Lepus (Volume 9, January 2024).

"Midnight Orchid" and "Flower" first appeared in
Litmora Literary Magazine
(Issue 3: Flower Language Edition, May 2024).

"Good Years", "Red" and "Waking" appeared in Vroom
Literary Magazine (Issue 1, January 2024).

"Flower" appeared in Literary Cocktail Magazine
(Spring Issue 2024).

"The Art of Escape", and "Universal Laws" first appeared in
POETiCA REViEW
(20th Anniversary Edition, December 2023).

"Texas" first appeared in Gingerbread Ritual Literary Journal
(Vol 1.6 January 2024).

This book is dedicated to the memory of
Laura Lawless Burgess.

Table of Contents

The Art of Escape

Cages can be very complex
or very simple.
The trick is not the lock,
it is the integrity
of the emptiness.
A womb can be a cage,
or a skull.
A mansion can be a cage,
or an ocean.
Apprehension, the pressure of
a void that is too great-
creates a vacuum,
swirling whirlwinds where
there should be quiet, peace,
there is noise,
constant noise.
A frenetic tiger
paces his rounds, he growls.
Walls moan and threaten
to implode. Thoughts
gallop and careen.
Gods mutter. Devils argue.
Finally, the only sound is
one high frequency tolling.
The lights brighten until the
only color is white.
Deaf and blind,
a spirit cannot fly.
Overwhelmed,
locked in-
a body is a cage,
a mind is a cage.
What is the way out?
Where is the key to release the

energy of deep passions,
brave fantasies and true love,
the key that that will
transform matter into soul?

Vengeance

At 5:30 all that remains
are lavender tendrils draped
across the sky,
stone-washed angel hair
spilling from the clouds.
The disarray of the
afternoon is not evident.
The remains of the rape-
golden entrails-
look just like sunbeams.
Angels are androgynous beings.
I took her from the front.
You took her from behind.
There were no holes, so
we opened him with knives.
He screamed and the
sounds became birdsong
and rain.
We invited the whole world
to take a turn at our game-
the celestial Gang Bang.
Because nothing in heaven
could ever be wrong,
the angel lived on
and the painted sky changed
as you and I fucked
that sunset to death
before the helpless moon.

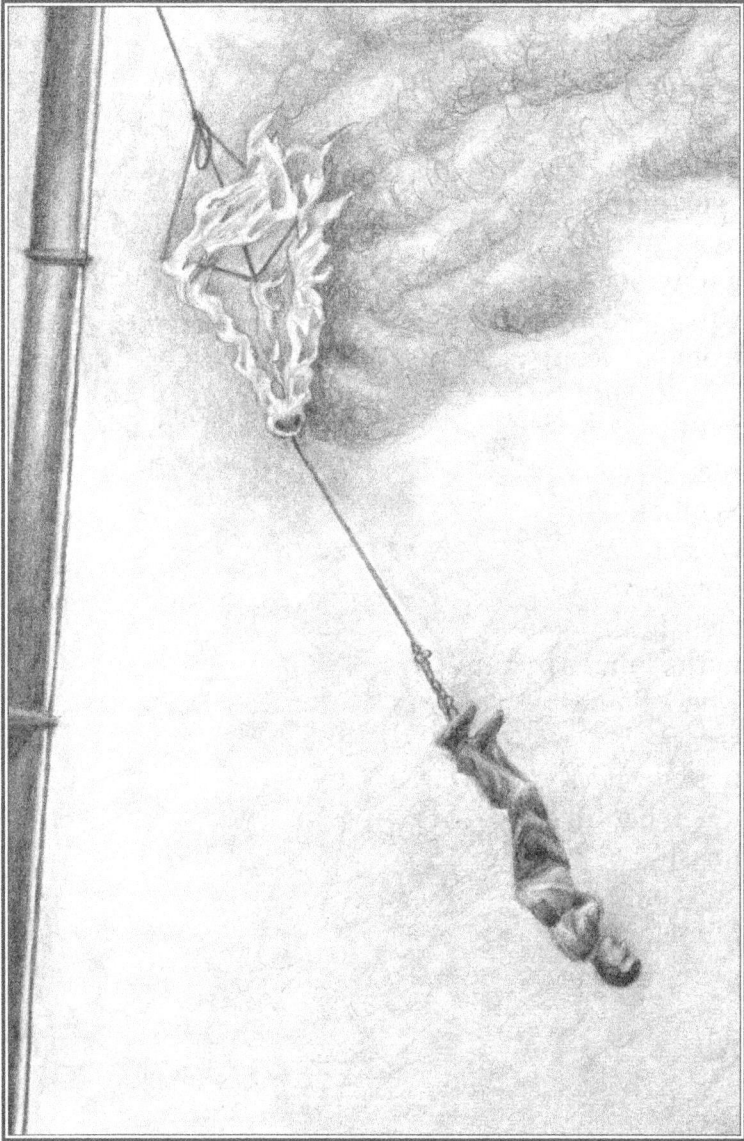

The Statue's Life

Statue of the
inner temple:
Willendorf fetish,
overripe breasts-
heavy with stone,
anonymous eyes,
vulva peeking out
from between
lush thighs.
Paralyzed by
rock-
Symbol.
Object.
Longs to
taste flesh
in the inner sanctum
where flames
shine-
but all who
touch her turn
to ash
and time sweeps
them away.

Night and Day

Sometimes I go out
in the dark,
avoiding the roads,
to meet creatures
of the night-
tail, feather, and claw.
Silence is their
sacred invitation,
a heart full of
wonder and free
of fear.
When I find the
first mighty wings
and glowing eyes,
the dripping jaws
in the starlight,
they invite me
into their corner
of moonlight and
whisper midnight
songs.
They wrap me
in rough fur and
bone necklaces
and baptize me
in blood.
Then they send me
stumbling home-
to sleep, to wake,
go to work, and
clickety-clack at
my keys and be
dumb and calm.

Snowfall

When you say
"I love you",
I don't believe it.
You say it too quickly-
like a fox darting
through the snow
and I know that
you have the
bones and teeth
of a selfish being,
surviving
with an eye for meat.
I know it isn't right.
Yet I stay awake
thinking of you
night after night.
I write you poetry-
words that will
last long after
your tracks
have disappeared
in the white.

Universal Laws

I've never met
a loyal person-
but I know if
you drop a dime
off the Empire State Building
it always falls down.
I've watched flesh disintegrate
like paper-
but I know that it's not gone,
it's only changed form-
to smoke in the air,
a wave of heat,
neurons flipped to stick in memory.
I've never told the whole truth,
but I know if it rains long enough
we all drown.
I've tested all kinds of books, stories,
religions, and philosophies and what
they profess. The laws of science and
math are the only things that have
turned out to be constant and true.
So I trust that time will march
forward for me and you. One
day our species will be extinct.
All these words we speak and think
will long since have returned to the
swirling energy pool. Even so,
I love you.

Valentine's Day

Valentine's Day state of paralysis-
I cannot feel my limbs.
I dreamed of them again-
my husband and children.
How long until the feeling returns
to my fingers and toes, until I
can move my neck, find a pen?
They aren't coming back.
The house is empty. There are
rivers, mountain ranges, and law
libraries in between us.
Loss can be like that cyclone in
a drain, continuous, then you
can't follow it down the pipe
to the ocean, you're left
shivering, watching, wondering.
"Be in the present, don't ruminate."
My present is this-
dreams of being happy with
a family that doesn't exist.
Waking, unable to move,
detached from pain and
its causes- writing about it.
Don't ask why, why will
kill like arsenic.
Why has no answers or reasons.
Why is a great twisted circle that
falls back on you again and again.
It helps a little to think of poor hurt
animals or people with bigger problems.
Maybe I can help them. If I can just
get out of bed and make these arms
and legs function. One more time.
I don't know why I'm still alive and

I don't believe in Father God with
his convenient list of reasons.
I am still here on Valentine's Day 2015.

How I Get Out of My Rope Ties
By Harry Houdini

1. The sailor boys, whom I had seen before, had the time of their lives tying me to that chair. And not one of them observed the sort of shoes I wore.

2. Upsetting myself, I was able to extract my foot from my Congress-Gaitor Shoe.

3. With both feet now out of my shoes, it wasn't difficult to extricate myself from the tie.

4. Until finally the loosened ropes dropped off me and I was free in 54 seconds.

Reproduction of image taken from "Ladies Home Journal," June 1918
– Written by Harry Houdini

Midnight Orchid

The sleepy flower feels
her dizzy hour begin
slipping, the dissolution-
soul's malnutrition
from tainted earth and
drunk moonbeams that
do not let chlorophyll flow.
Her violet reds gather in folds.
Bloom is beginning.
She can't wake up
to greet the sun.
She'll be a funeral rose,
brightening death.
The shy harlot of a staid garden,
transient, pollen like gold dust
on swollen lips, soft to resist
insect protuberances that dip
into sweet resinous nectar
kept secret from all but one,
the shadow son.
He brings a steel gun of
ultraviolet to coax her to bloom
at night with gamma frequencies
beyond man's sight, blast into
fractals, a queen of
psychedelia that no one else
sees, her arms multi-fold, spraying
petals through galaxies, her
fragrance freed to the sky,
intoxicating midnight bees.
The world inverses its photography.
She screams her true name
in his neon forest dreams and
he keeps it secret. He knows if he

takes a flower it dies, it cannot
breathe, so he leaves. The sun
opens a wary eye and the day's
disbelief begins. She closes off,
draws up, enfolds her spells to
sleep through the dangers of light-
each day a reckoning before
each night.

Sexual Favors

Always open your
mouth a little wider
for the boyfriend,
for the husband
Always sink a little
deeper in your crouch
of gratitude, popping that
ass in the air.
Always find a secret
refuge just for him,
a sexy sigh only he hears-,
and it becomes a trap
of his sexploitation,
his superiority,
his authority to do
as he pleases-
bestowed by you.
Always the relationship drains-
It seldom replenishes,
never fulfills.
Always remember to cover
your teeth and breath slowly
through your nose while
he grabs your skull.
Always remember the
taste of his cum is his life force
passing to you. You never spill
a drop.
Always hold rapt to his
war stories, laugh at his tired jokes.
Always know the balance
of the sighs and blows,
the ebbs and flows

the rapes and interrogations
of marital relations.
You always go back to the crime
scene looking for clues.
But the boyfriend/husband knows
not the way of love- only the way
of ownership and value and to that
he will be true. Your soul may come
up lost as long as your body
is not missing.
The only true love is free love.
But are there dark submissive tendencies
in your cavewoman DNA?
Do you secretly want to be
unequal,
carried away,
impregnated,
transformed into a slave
for a little bit of warmth and feed?
And will that powerful
instinct allow rough treatment,
exploitation, abuse, a whole
world of misery just to preserve
that pair bond? Just to get a few
precious sperm?
Just to bear children and have a home?
Always you see the same story.
It's even been my story too.
I'd like to write the story anew
beginning today.
Remember each soul is free.
No one owns you.
Each act of sex can be a declaration

of freedom, a liberation of self,
and a burst of creation whether
it is with a man or not.
Why do them any favors?

Wanted: Exorcist

Maybe I can starve this demon out.
Maybe I can smoke him out.
Maybe I can pray him out.
Maybe I can fuck him out.
Then he'll stop telling me,
"That's a perfect bridge,
Come back and jump off."
"That's the right direction
to cut- a vein to mutilate,
an artery to kill."
"That's the right belt to
hang yourself from a door
like Robin Williams did, XXL."
 "That's the maximum dosage
of acetaminophen. You would
triple it."
This demon's been at me awhile
Sometimes he's silent so long
I think he's gone.
Then he whispers- do it!
Then he mutters- do it!
Then he screams- DO IT!
I blink and I see myself sticking
my pen knife in my throat
I turn away quickly, feeling
puke in my throat. I grab the
little knife and shove it in
the back of a desk drawer,
mutter shut the fuck up.
I won't go to your places.
I won't gather your objects.
But sometimes, when I'm alone
and weak, I do. Sometimes having
those razors, that rope, that belt,

feels comforting.
Because the pressure of decisions,
even what shampoo to choose,
has crashed my system-
His voice is certain, commanding
He has an ultimate purpose for me.
He has the goals I've lost.
I know he is a monster from my own
chaos- no more real than the God
that abandoned me long ago.
If he is real then it must
be a hungry hell- desperate for delicious sinners.
If the Catholics are right I can't give in.
But I've got no evidence of afterlife.
Only demons.
I want to become good and
whole before I die- to live a meaningful life.
If I die by my own hand I'll be the nightmarish ghoul
of children's broken hearts, not to mention my caustic
ectoplasm splattering
onto parents and friends, burning
their lives with my toxic waste.
So how can I silence this demon -
Mother, Daddy, Doctor, Reverend?
I have lost my mind, see and hear things, and this
facade of sanity is critical to the survival
of six people who depend on me- yes, me! -
to provide, hold it together.
How do I defend us when I am not strong?
The demon cups his claws and
sings his tender evil into my ear, knowing to strike
when I am lonely and weak.
Do demons ever die?
Can they be silenced?
If I am determined to survive will I live a life of torture?

Red Flag Day

The beach is
crowded, packed
with chairs and
umbrellas, expectant
lotion-lathered
children in water wings-
but the Gulf is
beating the white sands
down with
a vengeance-
huge rip currents
and white caps
on these usually
calm shores.
Only an adventurous
few brave the waters
for a brief
"I dare you"
kind of play
and I too
have to try my
mettle against
those roiling waves,
to feel that
kind of power
behind me
all around me. . .
pulling me
pushing me
tossing me
like a toy.
Its Nature-
The thrill of its
tangible,

real experience,
immediate,
greater than me,
pure and true.

Spheres

Bobbing along in an unreality bubble,
I can still observe reality
beyond the rainbow residue.
I'm still aware of the great
sucking hole driving the
expansion of our universe.
Yet within my bubble of unreality,
pain is just another sensation
I greet with curious observation-
testing its gain, volume, and balance.
Blood is beautiful like diamonds, like water.
Glittering until it clots, I fear it not-
I wish for its release, its flow, its taste.
I want to paint its thousand crimsons.
Within my bubble I ingest herbs, wine,
mushrooms, pills, and nightshade.
The air comes in blue shock waves.
Bugs crawl along the window frames.
Faces appear and disappear in walls.
I remember every song I ever heard.
I seek out paper and pen.
No one comes inside my bubble.
Sometimes I'm there for a day,
a week, or more. I see all the little
people scurrying around in the real world.
I can answer them, but it can take
a while. My eyes are far away.
I do not choose when the bubble descends
or rises. Here it is now and I can only
describe it – never tame it or name its
purpose. Perhaps I just wanted you to know
where I go when I look away and don't

join the conversation. Perhaps you have a place like this too. Or am I the only person trapped inside these spheres of the unreal? Are they the harbingers of an unwell mind? Or are they a mysterious gift from an unknown isle?

Diamond Fire

Are you a wildfire
fast to catch,
rapid to rise,
burning everything
in your sight?
Or are you the fire
that burns long
and hard, deep in
the Earth, arousing
mountains?
I'll only know if
I let you burn me,
If I let this spark ignite-
But the truth is
the air is so hot
I'm vaporized.
There's no hope of
remaining unscarred.
No hope for landscapes
remaining uncharred.
If I must burn I will
know the hottest fire
at the center of the Sun
and some have called
it Hell, but I will
call it Heaven.
I will walk through your
fire unharmed and carry
your flame in my palm
to the stars-
If your fire is strong enough,
long enough,

hot enough
to burn and twist
my beautiful heart
into an invincible diamond.

Bump

When I interact with you,
my mind hits a mute button.
The chatter of the world is drowned.
Distractions are out-of-focus.
My eyes pinpoint a tunnel
as my guts shrink up.
It's hard to focus on words-
your language or meaning.
All I hear is your tone-
Is it threatening?
I hold my distance with you
as I would a viper,
to avoid both its
strike and its hypnosis.
Then after you are gone,
it takes the world awhile to
return to normal-
the focus of my vision,
my fight-or-flight
adrenaline,
the quality of sounds-
as if a shark bumped
me on a swim.

Flowers and Butterflies

Around nine years old
I became aware
that I possessed
certain attributes-
a curve of the lips
a brightness of eye
a pert little body-
that made me a
chosen flower,
plucked from among
countless others, to be
set in every exotic bouquet
on display.
But it's all a lie.
I'm still a simple flower
and I don't know
why all my love
turns to hate,
why I cannot bear
being stared at, my
fragrance inhaled.
I just want to be a
thorn or a nettle or
a cactus or a grand old
haunted tree full of raven
secrets and long-gone
tongues of lightning.
It must be I am too

full of life to disguise
myself.
My honey brings
bees, my urn of
nectar drowns the
lesser Insects, and a
cloud of gold dusts
the victorious.
Either that or I am
a Venus fly trap,
hungry for meat,
an illusion, alluring
only for deceit.
But I worry that no
one has ever seen
the real me and that
no one ever will.
Because what matters
most is that I'm pretty,
not what I ever said
or wrote.
A butterfly is no better
than a moth but a moth
earns no poetry,
no delicate tattoos
on ladies' ankles.
No admiration or envy.
This garden is full of fools.

I am not pretty.
My flower breathes
a song to the pool
where the butterflies
drown.

Mortality

Sometimes I feel every bone in
my skeleton grind.
Sometimes I see through my
pale skin.
All the delicate ribs and succulent
bits of lung clinging-
There is nothing in the mirror
but a gape-eyed skull,
its horrible grin reminding
me that I am death walking
in slow motion,
that vanity is a hilarious joke,
that I will soon be gone
and there is only a little
time to sing this song.
My bones make
secret catacombs.
I will be a sculpture,
a fossil, a relic,
a mystery when
humans no longer exist-
when new gods
come find me and
wonder what sort
of monster man was
before he burned the world.

La Brea

I am attempting,
for the sake of experiment
to draw my gaze away
from the yawning darkness.
But it's magnetic, fascinating
like a festering wound- endless.
I don't even feel the
beginning of the necrosis
that creeps over my fingers
as my eyes become fixed
and dilated, as a demon
latches to my intestines
mocks my heartbeat,
reminding me-
Come back
Come back
Come back and look again-
Look at all the aborted, beheaded,
twisted, destroyed, raped,
Holocausted, murdered hands
reaching for you. . .
the hacked-off limbs of
angels who lost the war
with Lucifer,
the piles of gold teeth and
hair pieces leftover from
the Jews who are now
windblown ash, who prayed
to God, but God was too busy that
day to save them from the gas.
All of it is too sticky like tar-
too real, blacker than black.
It pulls me back.
Once I look,

once I see that
cancer and viruses
are a fitting death
for an oblivious, selfish species-
No more, no less than
another weasel-like mammal that followed
the dinosaurs- that will come
and go like all species do
and so will its Art
its Technology
its Civilization
its God
its Poetry.
Its black hole and graves will gape.
This was my attempt at
writing myself away from
the La Brea pit of bones.
To maybe use this pen to
enlighten or lift my friends-
But it seems I was not meant
for that- it seems I was sent
to warn- Like Odysseus I
went to the Underworld and
came back. I have seen Hell
and brought you a piece of it.
You needn't die to see it,
to know its awful secret.
You need only look,
Seekers of Truth, who
dare and debauch yourselves
in that pursuit-
Ask yourselves if you will
cross any boundary- even if
you don't like what you see.

Nietzsche said it best-
'Beware that, when fighting
Monsters, you yourself do not
become a monster. . .for when
you gaze long into the abyss.
the abyss gazes also into you."

Pinball

I haven't cried a real tear
since I've been here.
Then today came
the deluge.
I've kept my heart
in a strong box,
carefully locked,
encased in layer after
layer of black lace.
My tears are blue.
Now all the layers
of lace are ripped,
the locks are picked.
My heart's pinned out
in a full vivisection
for the exposure
of pink secrets.
Its tender little
reflexes tested.
Yes, this nerve still
causes an electric
reaction all
the way up to her
confused brain.
Remember it,
It has multi-fold
purposes for the
objective scientist

or the opportunist
seeking ego-fulfillment.
Doctor, would you please
cauterize this nerve like you did the
tubes to my ovaries?
Cauterize the nerve
between my head and
heart that makes me
believe in someone who
holds me, kisses me, cums
in me, and repeats?
That nerve in my heart that
makes me feel something
more than biology, that makes
reality so painful when he's
really just pushing buttons-
playing with my brain like
a pinball game
to hear my sounds pinging,
to see my rows of lights flashing,
to find out if he can beat his all-time
high score and get one last free play?

Red

The sunshine
pushes its way through
the waft of my black
curtains, around the
seams and edges.
I see it, feel its
persistence
in mid-morning.
I think of how I
enjoy watching myself
bleed like the sunshine-
in punctures,
injections,
star patterns,
slices.
It's that persistence.
The persistence of life
that amazes me-
the fire, the blood,
the radiance of stars.

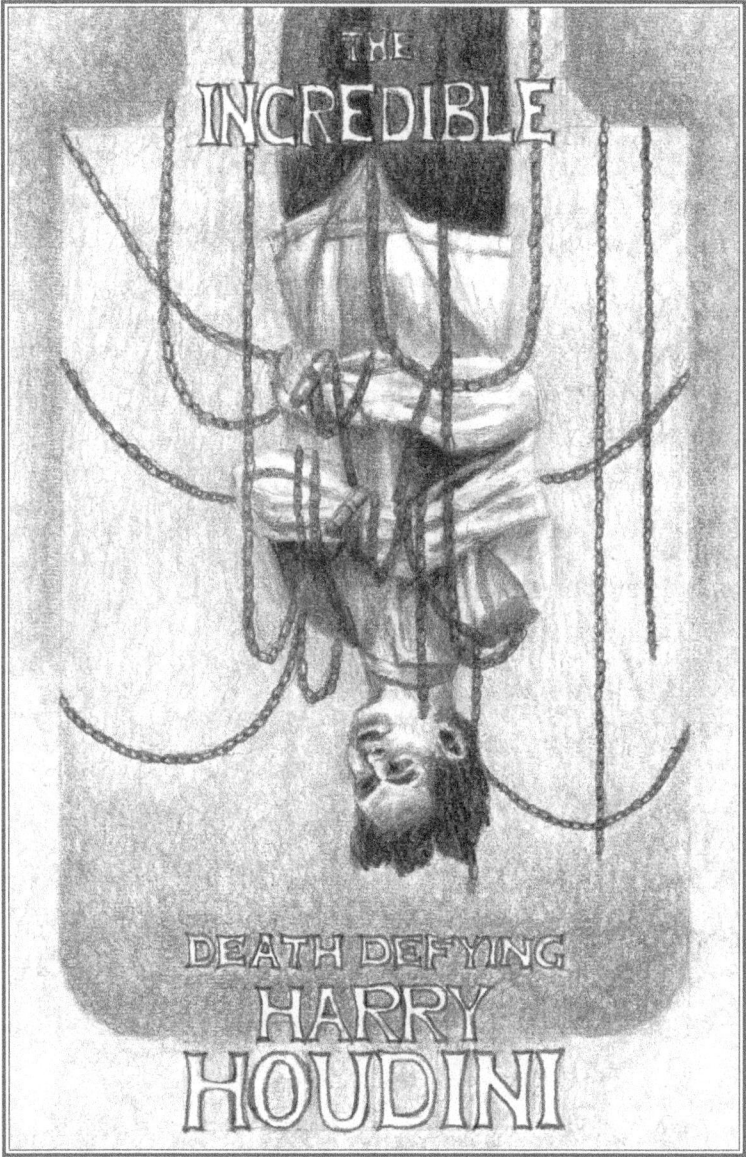

THE
INCREDIBLE

DEATH DEFYING
HARRY
HOUDINI

Among the Rushes

Today her silken prayers have become lost in the
rough leather corset of misunderstanding,
cinched tightly against pinched flesh and held breath.
High heels make that ass look just right.
Shoes that hurt are the soul of beauty.
What are bare feet running through the night?
The skinned knees and splinters from strange trees,
the tangles? She shouts down at passing men,
"Come away, O human child!" Bound faery,
trapped essence smashed into a push-up bra
with lipstick on her teeth again, a lost
cracked cell phone by her hand,
as ants surround her legs.

Texas

The real country boys
sip wine straight
from the bottle.
They remember when
the grapes were crushed
and Jose cut his arm
on the door. . ..
-the wasp stings.
Texas is a harsh place.
Nothing grows
here but
by sheer respect,
by venomous virtue
of life sprung from
deep wild roots
flung out among
wildcats' cries and
desiccation,
wasted wishes,
almosts,
coulda beens,
streams that
nearly made it
to the ocean
but trickled out.
We begin again
and again here.
It is a holy spring
surrounded by
a sentinel
of bones.

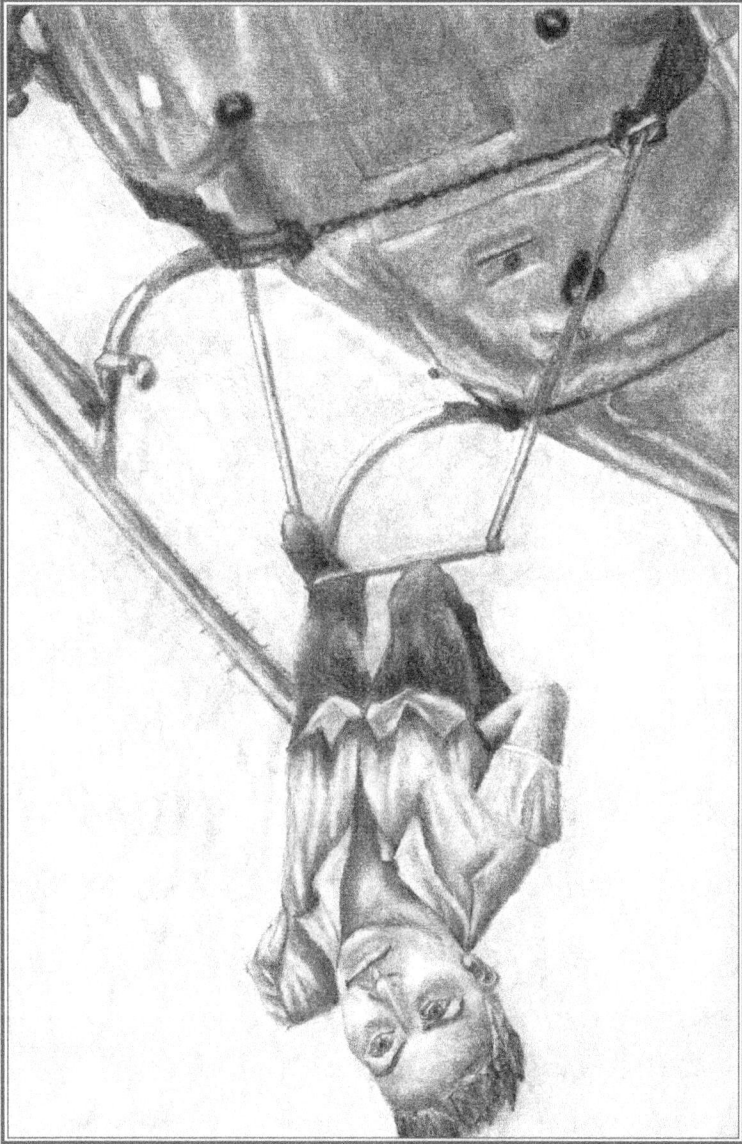

Whiplash

Whiplash
Shout
Eat
Desire

Fragment
Reach
Fuck
Stain

Gunshot
Table
Sphere
Heart

Trumpets for the pain.

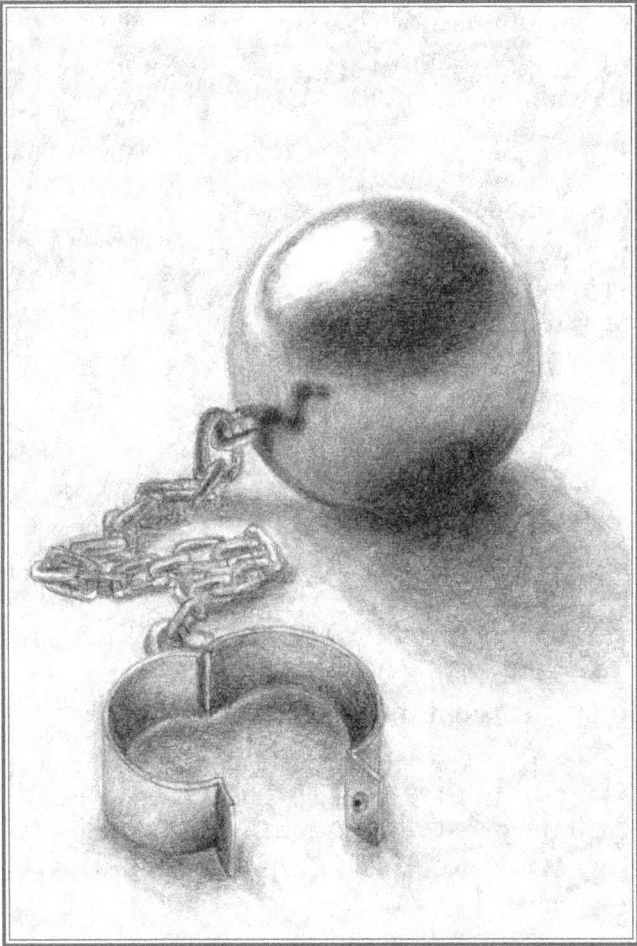

Good Years

Pennies are brown and dirty.
They stink of bus stops.
They will never add up to
a million dollars no matter
how many you collect in jars.
It's bad luck to throw a penny
away so I always bend down
when I sweep one up.
I've heard it costs more than
one cent to make a penny now
and that they are not even
real copper (but I haven't been
to Snopes to check this out).
If you name a girl Penny,
I'm not sure what you expect from her.
Sometimes at work, I take a
filthy corroded one, where you
can't even recognize Abraham Lincoln
and drop it in a jar of 10% nitric acid for
an hour- then it pretties up
like the day it was minted and all
the grime of the decades dissolves
away, all the pockets exchanged, dirty hands,
and register drawer dust- it's gone now
and I see a date-
1957- was it a good year?
Pennies are like us.

Bad Dreams (Crimes of the Mind)

I dreamed of murder,
vehicular slaughter of an innocent-
a petite young girl
who attracted my husband's eye.
Only I haven't been married to him since 2007.
We were together again.
I don't remember the murder itself,
just driving the bloody dented
car into the garage and going
upstairs to pass out.
Then waking the next day to my
father matter-of-factly washing
gore off the bumper with a garden hose.
I went out again the next night
and kidnapped a red-headed infant girl
to be my precious only daughter.
Smothering in coats and blankets,
I couldn't breathe in a classroom by the
sea on shaking docks. I finally got my pants off
and I seduced the engineering professor
because I knew he had a good job.

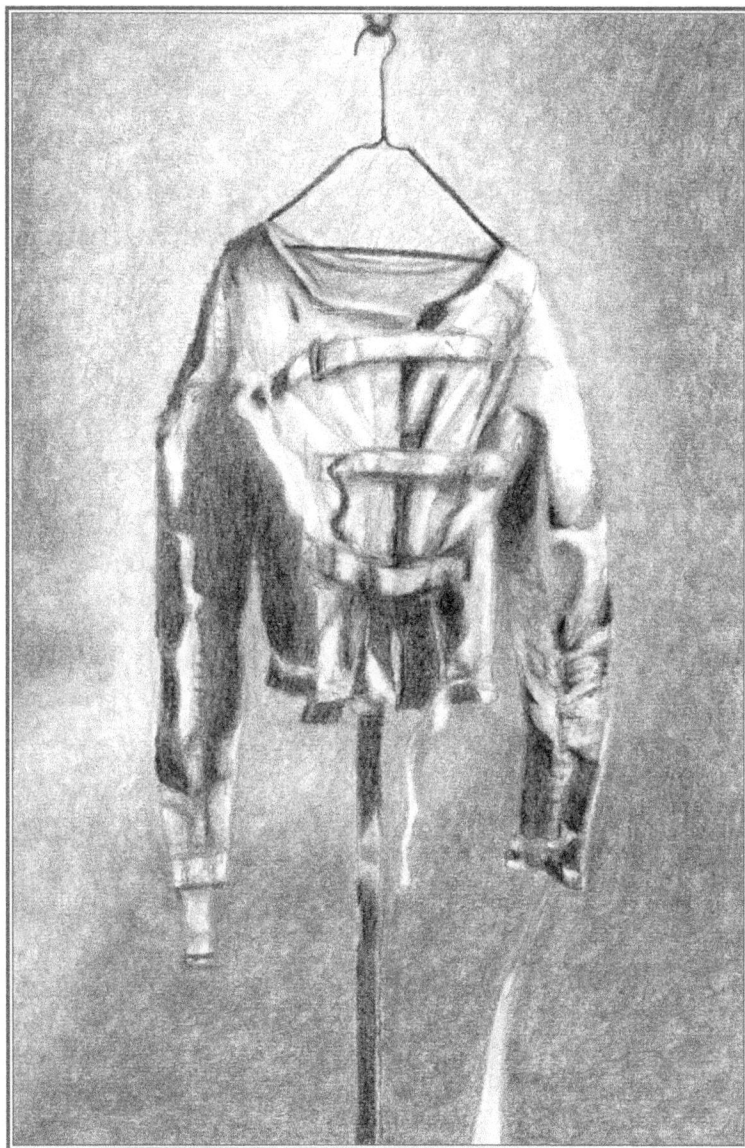

migraine

magnets misaligned
stirring the molten
electric core to the
turbulent counter-current
sudden tectonic shifts
and cranial twists
the sparkling metal mist
resists comprehension
the tension of snarled
wires on fire with green
evil and corrosive sparks
the heart cries talk
lips frostbitten
fingers bluelocked
the poles of the earth
reverse in shock
radiance blinds and
sonic waves deafen
every struggling quark
no organosynthetic thought
all is lost to the neural cauldron

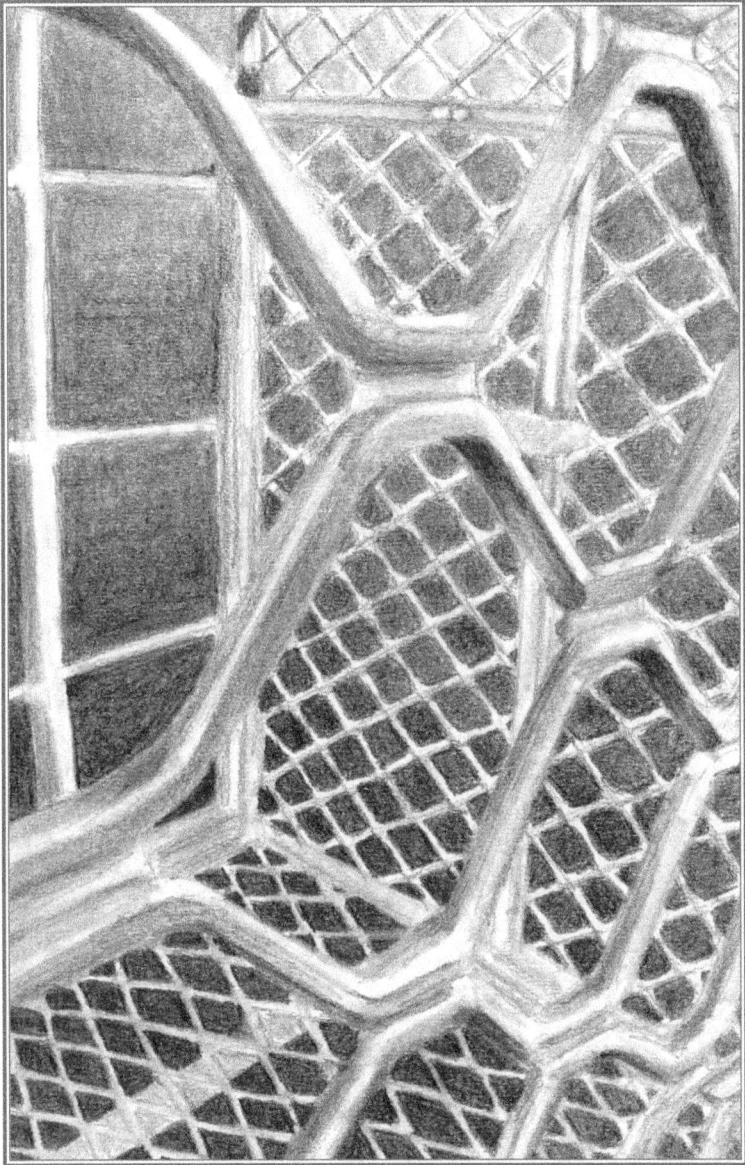

Waking

This is not real life.
This is the Dream.
I can prove it.
I'll set fire to anything
and it will not burn.
I'll step off a cliff
and drift slowly
to the ground.
These people
are not people.
I'm sure of that.
They are carbon clones
behind a mask.
Cut them and they
will not bleed.
Touch them and they
are cold.

The Beach

First, there were great dragons and
sea serpents, an enormous death-
mirror in the squid's eye
embraced in blankets of tentacles.
Then, the giant birds descended
to pluck the scaly Lords from
their ocean, tangled in talons
and solemn beaks- they were
carried to the land to be eaten.
The eyes of the dragons minced
with the fertile earth-
diamond scales strewn across
her moist brown belly.
Then, God came with his
semen of rain to make her complete
-full of reptilian flowers that
blossomed poison teeth.
These flowers smiled at me,
begging, "Pluck me! Quaff me deep."
You cannot hear the souls crushed
beneath us as you rape me to pieces.
I am pregnant with a thousand
stories. I wander the earth
drunk with bastard mysteries.
Every time I open my mouth to
speak, they rush forth- motley
armies of snakes, flowers, beasts,
unraveling, determined to
avenge their stolen mother-
streak the slime of time
on every shining leaf.

Every shore of washed-up secrets
is strewn with
detritus of the orgy,
the cannibalistic ritual,
the consummation.

Never Publish

Why do I cum when
I cut myself,
or when my lover burns me?
What kind of special creature
are you, that I have opened this
book, to share these words with you?
Not a judge,
Not a critic,
Not a doctor,
Not a policeman,
Not a father,
Not a husband.
Maybe you are someone who knows
what a woman like me is for,
what she can do,
or maybe you just stumbled over some
crazy tripwire in the dark and have no idea
what you've got into.
If you came to me because you know
what I am, then show me
you know the irony of my submission.
Show me you know how much
more love can slice and burn me than razors and flame.
Find out how love makes me cum
like Zeus ramming Hera's
milky twat with his thunderbolt.
Potency, power, passion will shake houses down
and move the seas.
Lightning frees the rain that slams into every
pore. Love like that will kill you quicker
than self-inflicted slices and burns,
it's a double overdose and it takes two
to open the door.

Toxins

There's a limited amount
of any poison
that the human
body can take
before you
succumb.
But if you build up
your tolerance slowly
you can take more
and more of a toxin-
amounts that would
be lethal to others
even, and yet you
continue to function.
This applies to
the psychic kind
of toxin as well
as the physical
kind.
Some people have
ingested more,
can ingest more,
continue to ingest
more, and go back
for more,
not knowing
they are on the edge
of what could kill them.

Organ Donor

Trammelwise, the surgical
dismemberment of eyes,
sliding lights,
favors to the young
surgeon who selects
the probes, a dissection,
a corpse's first
message to decode.
There remains,
the flow inside -
a being cold
and still alive
paralyzed, mute, splayed
unwilling to ascend.
Be tender with the
bone saw.
Show love with the
scalpel's edge-
Scientist, surgeon,
until the shell collapses,
the face sinks in-
Until the gravedigger comes,
vile and intrepid, a hero
bringing stew for worms.
The horror of the heart
remains, preserved in ice-
a heart that will
beat inside another.
Hearts are used twice.

At the End of the World

At the end of the world,
we get off the bus
and there is California,
bathed in silver mist.
At the end of the world,
we walk toward the ocean
on a pink dock and see
a golden bridge at the
edge of the blur.
At the end of the world,
shining people ride camels
and giant tigers into
frothing white waves.
The mist keeps the
sun from burning.
At the end of the world,
you take my hand
and I stumble.
We fall together
in a heap of limbs.
I'm on top of you
in the slush.
I laugh and say,
"This isn't for us."
At the end of the world,
we turn around
and walk back into
the harsh desert,
the blazing sun
and temples
on the fringe.

Reflection

Hanging with me is like a game
of double dare or truth-or-dare
or even Russian roulette sometimes.
I asked myself objectively
if I would be my own friend,
and I said, only if I was the
kind of person who liked
scary movies and roller coasters.
But it's not all about screaming
and adrenaline.
It's about laughter too, and highs
and edges.
Are you the kind of person
who likes that, who likes
to test. . . the limits?

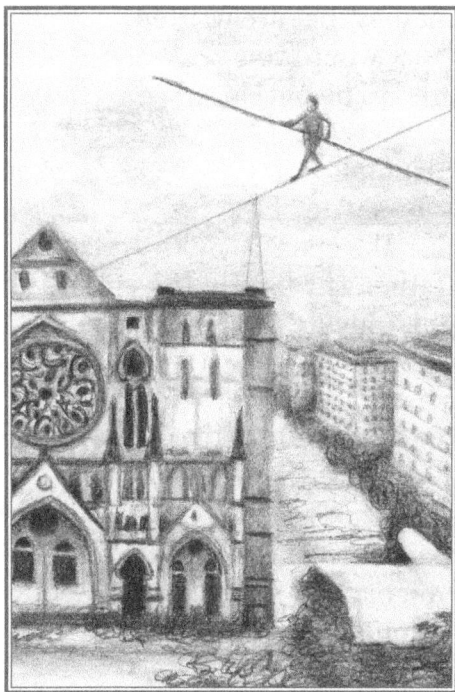

Rides

Pain and pleasure
are amusement park rides.
The larger mysteries concern
me- birth, creation, atrocity.
There is some evidence
I've already died.
In fact, that it was you that
killed me and I am
a form of ghoul bound
to this earth in damnation.
The fathoms of promises
echo to you, darling those
rising corpses, flooded verses,
vegetative half-rotted
illegible tombstones at the
bottom of our yesterdays-
I know the names that are written
in the cemetery where you
were supposed to be buried
by my side.
No one else can tell you
the hour or the shade of the
fevered infant, the cherished
daughter a father saw fade in the
morning light, only I,
your undead bride
walking the earth reeking of
fermentation.
I will drag you from whatever
resting place you choose
with fingernails torn and bruised
I will bury you back
where you belong, back on
the sunny hill of the past

where we were once alive,
riding the slides,
laughing at the shivers that
played up and down our spines
as we passed each solemn stone.

Depression

Lately I've been walking
along an edge, a jug of acid
balanced on my head,
my mouth glued shut.
I can only talk with my
hands and my eyes.
Limited movements
or words I can write,
the rations I'm issued
of freeze-dried time,
meals ready-to-eat.
Stories of far-off people's
suffering seem to dull
the edge of my own.
I pretend to be fine and
the fear that grows-
I defeat with an imaginary
super-self, capable of anything-
But who do I tell when the infected
edges of truth begin to ache and swell?
It's a tightrope act I've begun with
no net and I know the consequences
of collapse are catastrophic and colossal.
I'm not a prophet. I'm merely a
haunted girl who speaks with
beasts and ghosts, a Cassandra.
I'm an unfit human being.
No one can know my whole story.
Oh, how I ache to tell. If
I had a true friend in the
world who could read every page
of my soul these corpses would not
grow so much mold- this invisible coat
of bones would not be so heavy.

You would not ever smile
at me if you knew. You would
not love me, you would fear for your
own soul. And so I do not open my mouth
when the darkness is not under control.
I sleep it off for untold hours. I imbibe
in amnesia's flower. I bind myself with
magic to protect the ones I love and
I take a vow of silence, solitude, and
living death.

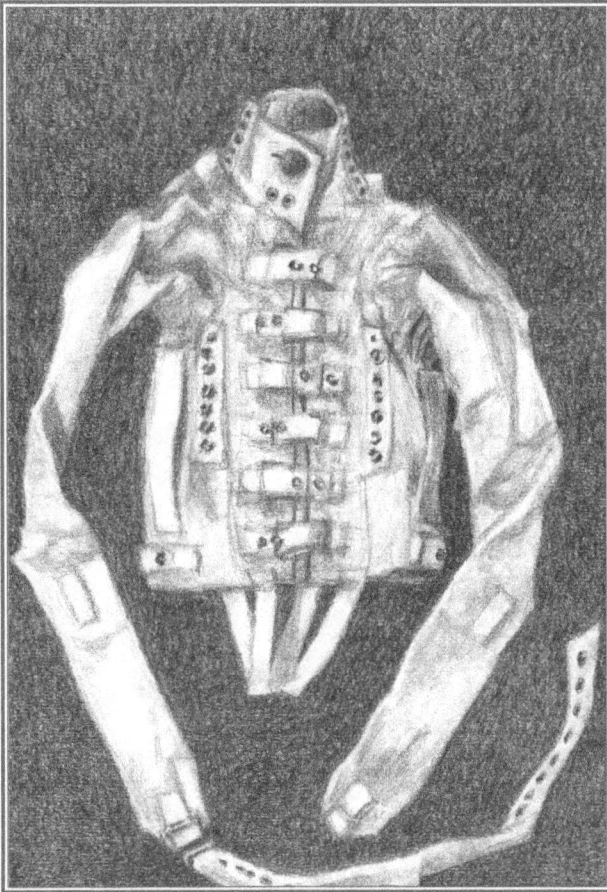

Emerald Coast

This cove is desolate,
a windblown hollow
of salty dunes
and straggling
pines, the hurricane's
eye too many times-
where man o'war drag
themselves on the shore
to die, glorious opalescent
tentacles a tangle,
flash of violet
worlds below the shallow
emerald waters.
Nothing was ever meant to
live here, nothing permanent.
People build houses of paper
and castles of sand.

Bad Girlfriend

Two alarms and a dozen
frantic texts ignored. . .
down in the fetal position
on the eyelash blue shag carpet . . .
I wish I could interact.
I wish I could unfold from
these wracking sobs and cramps.
Look at the strange almost-forty tattooed
brunette in the mirror- she frightens me.
She is unpredictable, unfamiliar.
And she looks like she can't dance.
I don't know what I might do when
I'm feeling like this- like a loose stick
of dynamite. Best to go to bed.
Turn off all sensation,
ubiquitous inputs causing interference,
static disruption of my inner balance,
my core sense. I'll turn off all the
lights and crawl into bed still wearing
the red hot party dress I was going
out in, a streetwise Sleeping Beauty
waiting for her Rock Star Prince.
I know I should call him.
I know there is love, faith, obligation.
But I'm frozen behind a wall of thorns,
guarded by a jealous gold dragon.
I'm in his castle's tallest keep, asleep
under a thousand-year curse and
I'm sorry for being a bad girlfriend
                    a bad daughter
                    a bad employee
                    a bad mother
                    a bad friend

71

Maybe it will be different when
I wake up again. Even this curse can
be broken.

Heavenly Body

Like a pulsar, I live
in the velvet depths
of space,
always cycling between
explosion,
disintegration,
always spinning-
sending off erratic signals-
flash images of memories,
constellations I hooked
together in menageries
of gods.
Holding at my core the
dense dust of the
original boom that started this
lonesome journey.
Hoping some creature
somewhere will
wish upon me as
I blink and that I
can deliver that wish.
It's simple to be such a thing.
It's elegant but it's messy
too when all the stardust
starts to fly apart
then suddenly it is
sucked back into the
framework of a being.
I'm often confused.
Often I don't remember things.
But I remember the wishes.
Every single one.
I suck and blow my

own essence in and out
of existence.
I skate along the edges of
this trap of light and dark
with a will
to continue and discontinue,
to love and hate,
to matter,
to be the brightest and darkest star
that ever burned the sky.

Traps

The darkest silhouettes
pass me sometimes.
Men beating other men,
lies,
frantic molestation
beneath smothering
blankets,
weirdness,
blindfolds,
         torture chambers,
prisons,
      hallways that never end,
repetition,
       sound of bones breaking,
rape,
lights out,
            alarms,
               smell of medicine,
    I must escape.

No one can live this way.
Captors must sleep.
Every door has a key.
No cage ever made
can contain me.
Slip out of my skin.

      Run.

Lamb's Blood

If there is a Hebrew God
named Yahweh
and he created me and mine,
then I am very afraid
of what that means.
You see, I've read the
Old Testament and the New
completely through-
and especially the Old one
is not very nice.
Yahweh sends plagues,
wars, demands infant
blood, floods worlds,
levels
city walls.
He smites people.
God the Father has his
favorites. He does not
love all his children the same.
Just ask Ham.
Just ask Cain.
Then comes the
New Testament-
Yahweh's grand plan to redeem
us- to allow his perfect
gentle son to die by slow
torture among thieves.
I ask you all-
if I belong to
such a God- should I
not fear his wrath-
and his love too?
And you- if I belong
to such a God- perhaps

you should not be my enemy-
if he will kill his own son-
what will he do to you?
He says he is the owner
of vengeance.
I tried to be an agnostic,
then a pagan, but He
came with great force
to remind me of the jealous
God I belong to- my parents'
dedicated me as a child.
Would all my vain ideas of
free will matter to such as He?
Ha! I am arrogant and I will
bear the full punishment of my
disobedience before I see the place
my One God has for me in the
millionth facet of his enormous
eye. If any god is real, it is the
jealous, mean, childish, war-
mongering, murderous, all-
powerful, white male God who
claimed me long ago,
disguised as a gentle lamb.
There is none, or there is He.
Believe in him or be punished.
Believe in him or be free.

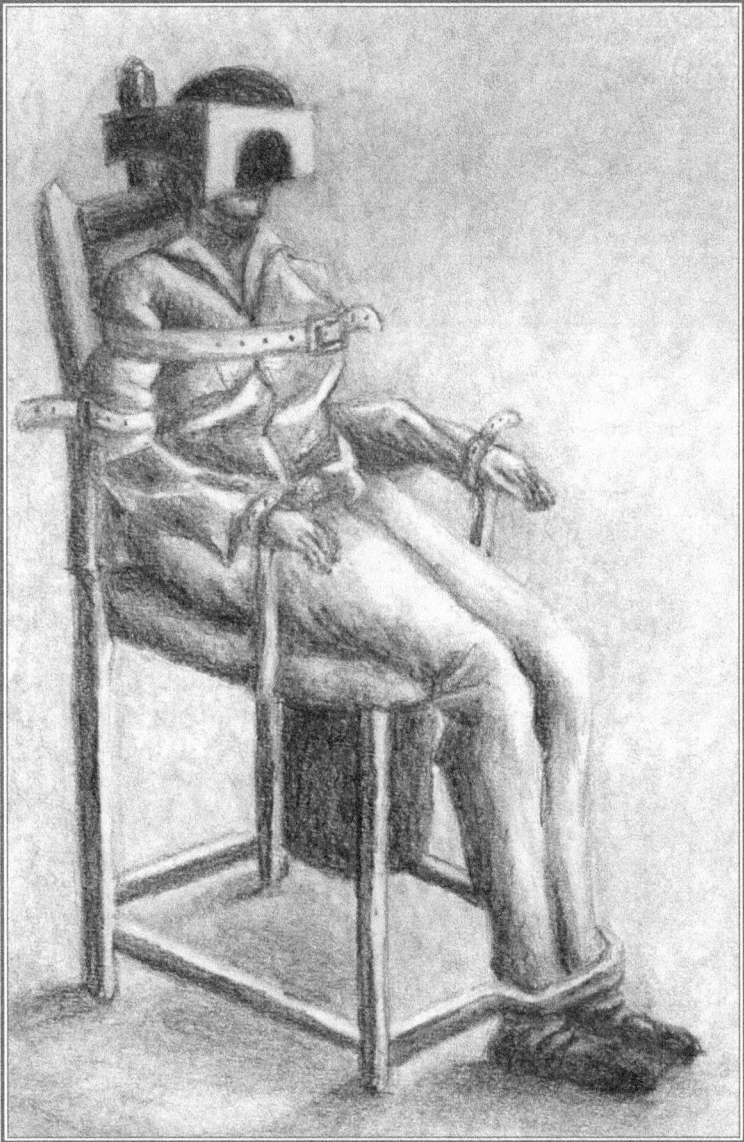

Locked Away

Cyanide is sweet amaretto.
The razor is a wet silver leaf.
The noose is a silk necklace of trust.
My final note is a melancholy tune
a night bird sings to the setting moon.
All these fragments of my suicidal wishes
have become locked in the enchanted
garden of my poem.

New Moon

Just let it go.
Let it flow
over you,
around you,
through you,
like a river
of black ink.
If you resist,
you risk drowning.
Just become at
one with the nature
of moons, cycles,
tides ebb and wane.
The beauty of
the new moon-
turning away
from bright shining
and letting darkness breathe
free at last,
unashamed,
tears of blood pouring,
leaving Rorschach tests
on the page to be
interpreted by more
objective parties.
Let the black wings spread
like the Shadow of Death,
comforting the least terrified
rabbit. Let it all collide.
Let it slide like paradise
in the Serpent's eyes when
he told God's truth.

Let it go.
Don't fight anymore.
It's not your War.
Stop being a metaphysical pawn
and dwell in the
black and white
equally-
to balance and be free
of this constant turmoil,
this bitter struggle.
Let this sadness
come and go,
like all things do.

Bitch/Slut/Whore

Here in the city
I put on
my slut eyes
and my slut
shoes, tremble
in the blue
light of the
stage as the
page flutters-
caricature
of Western
woman-
ready to
say something
dumb,
swallow some
cum,
feeling so
numb.
But what you
see is not
what you get.
I am deadly.
I am mother.
I am poet.
I am scientist.
The joke's on you.
I am the punk
rock whore
of the world too.
All these things-
but nothing
simple,
nothing trite,

nothing easy.
I fuck who I choose.
And that quality
in men is strength–
it's strength in
women too.
I won't cringe
before the words
bitch slut whore
anymore.
I'll say thank you.

Razor

The edge of existence
is upon us and it
is not abstract,
not pleasant,
not comforting,
not convenient.
It is the edge.
You fall off it-
that's the end.
You die.
No continuance.
You stay on the ledge,
secure, you continue
to open your eyes,
raped with photons-
your corneas
perceive the light.
So choose a
side of the edge
each day
until the last,
when even the unwilling
have their reluctant
souls cast to the other side.

Angel

Here I come
in the wild plasmatic
afterbirth of Earth's
spasms,
seeking that sensation
I feel at the edge,
icy wind as I'm falling-
9.8 m/s^2 isn't fast
enough for me or you
at the cliffs.
Let's accelerate beyond
the bonds of our
worldly mothers and fathers,
become angels in the
star harbors,
kiss God's giant feet
and carry his messages,
cut down evil doers
with invisible swords
and bring desperate
prisoners rainbows
through their bars.
We'll shield the innocent
and rescue the lost.
Then one day,
we'll rain fire on
Mother Earth.
You and I
will ride
each blazing
star into her
molten heart,
to embrace and
cleanse her of

humanity's infestation.
You and I
will be scarred angels
who take frightened
children under
our black wings
and carry them
to heaven.

Flower

Tonight, on a petal's precipice,
I do not desire doors open.
I wish to crawl along a wet stem
and fall into the cup of my words
where the effervescent poison
surrounds me, bubbles into
airways- my own fragrance,
heavy pheromones, funeral
garlands, Snow White's torn skin,
thorn's favorite innocent-
not a symbol of love,
this Rose Red,
an insatiable climber, a thief of light,
destined to drown in folds of darkness
between the
bright pink lurid lush
bait.
Impossible to capture alive-
impossible to sell, free to see.
I do not desire doors open.
I close my hungry mouth.

Descriptive Poem

(5 senses plus pain)

Pain shapes us like water on a mountain.

When it begins,
sensations overwhelm me.
Smell.
I become a bloodhound.
I can smell coffee brewing
three floors down.
I can smell the whiskey my
boss had yesterday morning.
I can smell that Clarice is wearing
a fresh Band Aid today.
Sound.
Oh how I hate
DOOR SLAMMERS!!!
They do not know the
agony they cause.
I want to scream,
"Shut the fuck up!"
at everyone, "Stop
stomping around!"
I can hear insects scurrying
inside my walls.
Sight.
Lights become so
bright they are unbearable,
Each photon a tiny diamond
edged dagger. The only hope
is to hide like a vampire.
Touch.
A roller coaster.
There is no solid ground.

It feels like you've been
gut punched or thrown about.
Taste.
Only taste remains-
sweet and salty and sour
are still reliable like the hour.
Why does my brain over-
amplify everything?
Then after the sensation
blast comes the
Pain.
It lasts one day to one week.
It feels like a taser going
off inside my head or an
auger being driven into
the center of my brain.

Sometimes the pain helps me
write poetry because
pain is more interesting
than happiness.

China

The new colors in the
expansive forests of bamboo
switched her sky with her soil,
low field crops drowning
in swamps of urban runoff
and shallow streams
were the tears of kings
who could never rule in a world
of modern democracies,
of politics, of United Nations.
They became criminals
and she became a detective
out among the mountains.
There was no fruit for queens.
The nervous birds became her
servants and the sky begged
the edge of the machete.

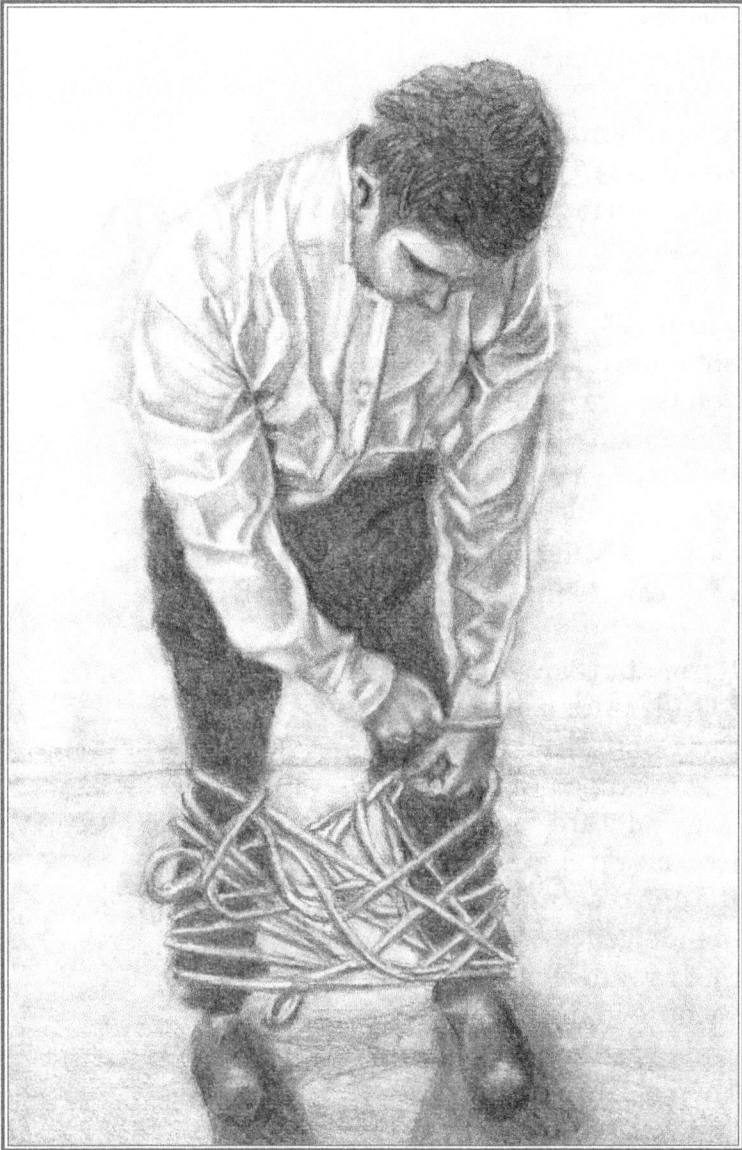

The Fountain

Wishes don't
have to make sense.
That penny you throw
in the fountain-
You don't have to
justify what you whisper
inside your head.
It already proves
you are illogical,
not quite an atheist.
You believe in the God
of fountains
and the Faery
of wishes,
or maybe you figure
what can it hurt-
to hope just for a second?
It can't hurt anything
to believe for a second-
this wondrous thing
might happen to you.
You really are special.
Dreams do come true.
It's only a second or two
of indulgence-
that reward center
synapse in the
brain flashes.
Then it's over
and you come back
to sense and your
empty hand
and you laugh.
Why not do it again?

Why not cash in
your whole paycheck
and fill the fountain
to its brim?
But it doesn't
work that way.
You move along
and dismiss it
as a whim-
the wish your heart
was so desperate
to say to someone,
but couldn't.
Now a secret-
because if you tell it,
it won't ever come true.
So keep silent,
and let that shiny coin sink
with your wish
to the bottom of the fountain
to reflect metal into sky.

To a Fighter

Busted lips
taste like passion.
Busted lips
taste like pride.
Busted lips
taste like
red hot words,
too many angles,
sibling rivalry.
Lick them raw.
They flake away in
pink translucent pieces,
bleed a little more.
The ghost of the giver,
the badge of the orgy.
By now it doesn't
matter who was right
or whether it was lust or hate
that delivered the blow.
All that matters
is that thumping ache,
that sweet mix of iron and flesh.
You are human after all.

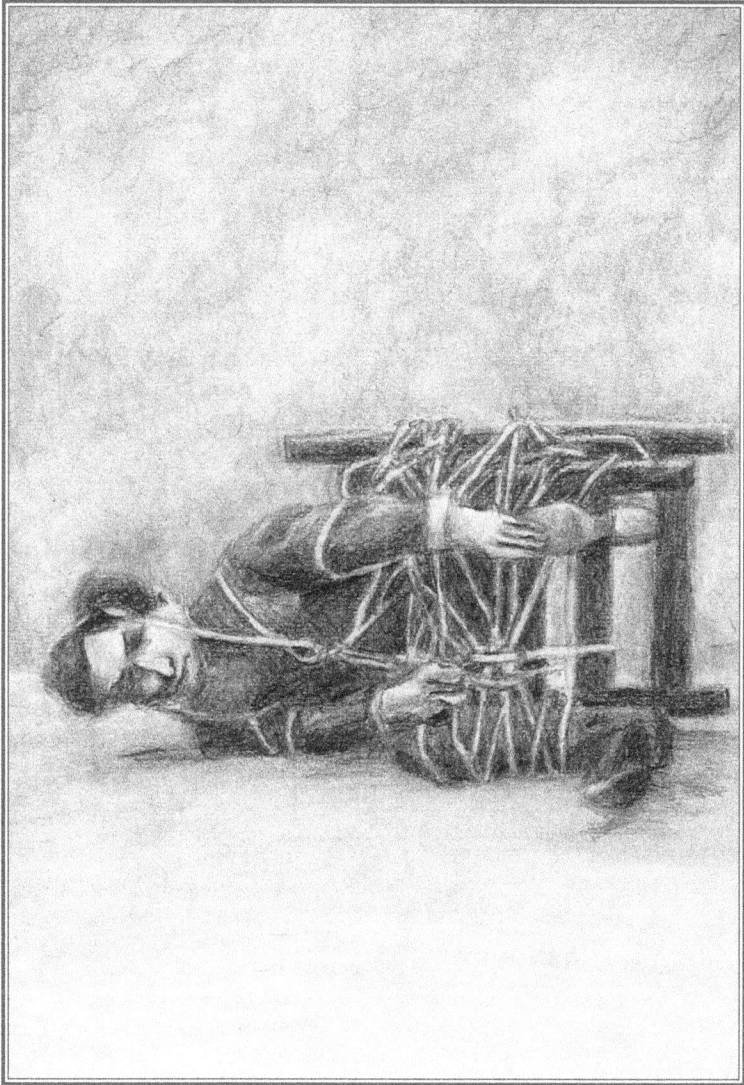

May

I could awaken-
reborn at the
center of a lotus,
unblemished by wounds-
green eyes eager to
receive earth's wonders-
heart ready to trust.
Would you love me then?
All I have to do is die
in this garden of delight
and wait for the spring rain.
The water and the sunlight
make dead limbs whole again.
I would be a new girl,
a virgin, untouched.
I could finally stop fighting.
I'd be beautiful enough.

Off Button

We trust our eyes
and ears as the
primary gates to
our existence-
but these can
be shut down.
Words, sounds,
and pictures
are formed by
our mind
and will continue
to exist in darkness
and silence.
Remove all
stimulus
and see what
emerges from
the echoless depths
of your mind.
They say drugs
alter the mind-
that the mind
can be tricked.
Not enough sleep,
not enough food,
a high fever,
and all our
neural networks
go blip.
Suddenly reality
isn't what we
thought it to be-

What if the world
of our imagination,
dreams, and hallucinations is
another facet of
reality that we
can't see sometimes?
Thoughts are
as real as
mountains and
as infinite as stars-
Just as energy
and matter
have a wave and
a particle form,
life is more than we perceive-
it is also what we dream.

Restless Brain

Caught in a storm
of nascent ideas with
the tips of knives
tickling my vertebrae-
alert and senses heightened,
the round fan as loud as
a tidal wave.
Time ticks by like
the seconds to lift off.
I feel phantom seat belts
and restraints, a pressure
larger than gravity.
I've got to break free.
The impossibility of
relaxation, the closed
insurmountable gates
of Nirvana, the laughable
teachings of Zen, please
tell me when the rabbit
will break free of the gate
and I can just chase until
battery acid drips from my
tongue and I'm
done done done
too exhausted to think
finally
I've silenced the seething mob.

The Urge

There are not enough moments of the
perfect intensity for writing.
I seize upon them with greed
and serve a table for the Muses.
I send dishes crashing to the floor,
search for pens like a pen fiend-
frantically discarding the
ones that do not write,
crawl on the floor, swearing, reaching
under dressers and beds.
Then bliss when the first line spills
and my mind knows some relief
from sorting all my thoughts and dreams
into patterns and codes of language,
to pass my time on earth,
to pass a message, with all the naïve
love of imagination an artist wears
like a badge, I say yes I am virgin innocent
in love with my art. I come when she calls.

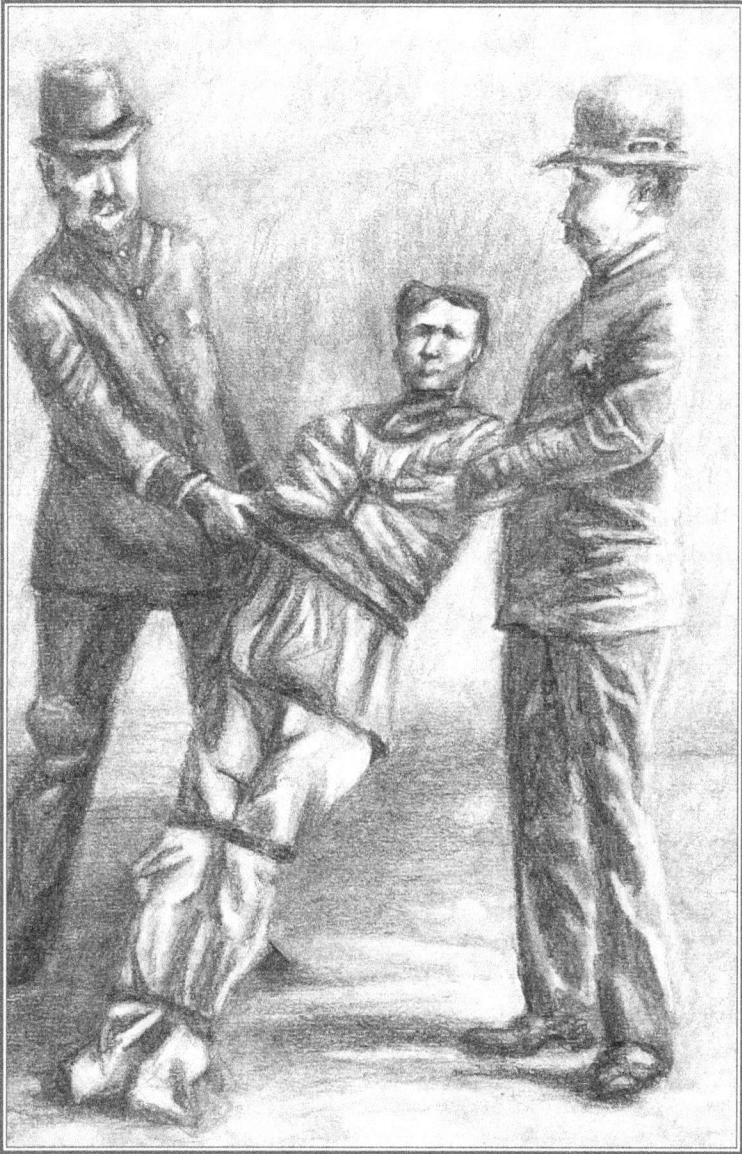

Forget me not

Forget,
forget me not.
Swirling mass of the hydra,
swollen sucking lips,
tentacle suction switch.
Forget,
forget me not.
Luscious, vicious,
precious viscous,
fluidic princess,
bountiful tips.
Forget,
forget me not.
Amazon aortic flip,
amniotic albino,
Aztec aberration.
Forget,
Forget me not.
Fallacious salacious,
ostentatious farewell
to these phantom
Barbie doll tits.
Forget,
forget me not.

Witch

Sometimes I feel
as gentle as a hippie
in her thrift store skirt.
But sometimes I'm ready
to blow up a depot and
make the fat men hurt.
Sometimes I'll laugh when
cat-called and provoked.
But sometimes I unleash
hell hounds on ignorant jerks.
Sometimes I'll let a man abuse me-
sniff, whine, and play the part.
Then one day I awake,
taze him,
and cut off his vital parts.
Sometimes I'm a sweet, soft,
cooing dove. Then others I'm
an orange cat who savors feathers
and blood. Sometimes I'm a
nature child who would harm none.
Then other nights I boil eye of newt
with black swan's blood and paint
glyphs on the wall.
Sometimes I believe in good, light,
truth, and love.
Other days, I believe in craven desire,
the Death Machine, greed, and disease.
I need Love betwixt and between.
I need Love when I am Good and
when I am Evil, just like Satan and God.
I don't need Jesus or rehab
or jail. I don't need torture, re-education,
or burning at the stake.
I just need eyes that

never look away. I need a friend
who believes not in mythology,
but in wretched, blessed human beings
in all their glories, all their mistakes.
I know I frighten people sometimes.
Sometimes, I frighten myself. But I know
all these sides of me are real.
I know that the witch men fear- is a woman
with the power to manifest reality from
her thoughts, words, and dreams.
And so it seems I am powerful and should
be hemmed in, labelled, counseled, confined,
and if necessary- destroyed.
I won't let that happen if I see it coming.
The spell I'm casting is one to be aware,
aware of the danger of being fully realized.
I am witch. I have been, and will be-
with or without the labels of society-
with or without safe haven- among you.

Vapors

Gasoline vapor ghosts
drift across the asphalt.
A rainbow hugs
the yellow haze.
Frenetic traffic, the nullified
citizens, glassy eyed-
they suck down corn syrup
and pollute the atmosphere
with Jurassic incense,
rich and deep.
I could become
the dancing vapors,
the rainbow,
the smoke,
black carbon transformed
on blue nitrogen seas-
unbound, untouchable energy
riding the Texas breeze-

Perfect Life

The first day you get out
of the mental hospital,
the lack of sickness
in the air is sweet.
You take it in,
you hold your breath,
grateful for little things-
the quiet click of
your keyboard,
a decent shower,
being able to shave unobserved,
being able to use a real pen.
But after awhile
you begin to think
of the people you
met within those walls. . .
wondering what
will happen to them-
Because the irony of
it all is that you meet
some of the best people
in unlikely places like
homeless shelters,
crazy houses,
and jails and some of
the worst people in
high society, politics,
and churches.
You see, what I value in
people is that bright light
shining in a tortured soul
that refuses to be put out-
despite the most
brutal circumstances.

Maybe what drives me mad
is that the rest of the world
can't see it and elevates
vain and obnoxious
people instead.
Every breath of happiness
and freedom I take is with
humble acknowledgement
to our human condition
of suffering.
I will never forget
those friends
and it is they that
make me grateful
for my experience
of a less than perfect
life.

The following (living and dead) escape artists, dare-devils, and performers inspired many of the images in this book:

Harry Houdini (1874-1926) - world famous Hungarian-American escape artist, illusionist, and stuntman. He originated and performed many death-defying escapes and stunts in front of amazed crowds including the Milk Can, the Chinese Water Torture Cell, Buried Alive, and the Inverted Straitjacket escape. Before he performed in a town, he would publicize his performances by challenging the local police department to lock him in, as best they could, in their jail overnight, with as many handcuffs and chains as they liked. Naturally, they would search Houdini beforehand. He would then emerge from the jail, unscathed, by the next morning. Houdini was one of the biggest celebrities of his time. He was also a lifelong debunker of the occult, spiritualists, and mediums. He died on Halloween of 1926 of a ruptured appendix after a student named Gordon Whitehead unexpectedly punched him several times in the abdomen. Houdini had previously boasted he could withstand the hardest punch a man could deliver.

Ormer Leslie "Lock" Locklear (1891-1920) - an American daredevil, stunt pilot, and actor whose popular flying circus caught the attention of Hollywood producers. At that time, he was considered the foremost aerial stuntman in the world. He starred in two films, "The Great Air Robbery" and "The Skywayman". During the second film, his plane crashed during a climactic dive and flew blindly into the ground, killing him instantly. The scene is still on the film.

Dorothy Dietrich (1948-) - an American escape artist and magician who is famous for shattering the glass ceiling for female escapologists. She is known for performing a Bullet Catch in her mouth and for being the first female to perform the Inverted Strait-jacket escape suspended from a burning rope. She also gained fame on television for sawing male celebrities in half. For many years she kept up the tradition of the Houdini seances in New York started by the magician's family as a tribute to the magician. Like Houdini, she crusades against mediums and spiritualists who take advantage of people attempting to speak to dead relatives. She has offered $10,000 to anyone who can contact the spirit of Houdini. Dietrich also operates the world's only continuous traveling Houdini Museum.

Philippe Petit (1949-) - a French highwire artist whose meteoric rise to fame started in 1973 after the unauthorized highwire walks between the towers of Notre Dame cathedral and the Sydney Harbor Bridge. Then in 1974 he illegally walked a highwire between the World Trade Center Twin Towers high above New York City, cementing his worldwide celebrity. Petit recently walked a highwire for the 50th anniversary of the 1974 performance at the age of 74.

Criss Angel (1967-) - an American magician and illusionist, currently considered one of the most suc-cessful in the world. He generates close to $150 million dollars a year in revenue in Las Vegas. Known for his hit television show MINDFREAK, he holds multiple world records and awards, including the world record for longest body suspension. In 2002, Angel spent 24 hours in a Chinese Water Torture Cell inspired by Houdini in the middle of New York's Times Square. He has performed other Houdini inspired stunts including the Inverted Straitjacket and a variation of Buried Alive in which he is buried in ice and snow.

Jonathan Goodwin- (1980-) - a Welsh former escape artist and stuntman who retired after suffering severe injuries, including a severed spinal cord, following a rehearsal for a 2021 stunt on America's Got Talent Extreme. Goodwin had previously enjoyed a successful career performing stunts on a variety of shows leading up to his 2020 finish as a semi-finalist on America's Got Talent. The stunt was supposed to be the Inverted Straitjacket escape, 30 feet in the air, suspended between two cars. The stunt failed and he was crushed between the cars as they caught fire. Today he requires the use of a wheelchair.

Dayle Krall (????-) - a Canadian escape artist known as the "Houdini Girl". She is famous for having mastered many classic Houdini escapes such as the Chinese Water Torture Cell, the Milk Can, and the Authentic Canvas Straitjacket. She is the only woman in the world who currently performs the Chinese Water Torture Cell escape in the original upside-down position, as Houdini did. In addition to inspiring several of the images in this book, she appears performing an escape in a poetry video for the Art of Escape narrated by the author.

Antony Britton (????-) - a British escape artist and stunt performer who became active in about 2012. He went on to perform many stunts for charity, including a famous stunt in 2014 where thousands turned out to watch him attempt the Inverted Straitjacket escape in the city center of Bradford. Later in 2015, he attempted the Buried Alive escape, making him only the third person to have attempted it in 100 years. The attempt failed and he had to be rescued.

About the Illustrator...

Tarynn "Di'Nnovati" Neary is an artist, entrepreneur, and intellectual born and raised in Albuquerque, New Mexico. She has pursued a diverse array of artistic media throughout her life - from ceramics, jewelry, and print-making, to mural-painting, piano-playing, and writing. She earned her fine arts degree from the University of New Mexico with a focus in bronze casting. She moved to Ohio for a job at a bronze sculpture foundry, where she worked through the height of the pandemic; she has subsequently worked in various arts production facilities and an art museum, all the while creating her debut sculpture series "Cycles of Fire". She now works as the print and marketing supervisor at a supply store, runs her own art store website, and art-based YouTube channel. In addition, she operates a hobby-scale houseplant shop. She accepts contracts and commissions as a freelance artist, including her commission to illustrate this book.

Find her at:
Website: https://www.dinnovati-art.store
YouTube: @dinnovati_art
Facebook: DiNnnovatiArt
Instagram: @dinnovati.art
Mercari: @red_berry_orchid

www.ingramcontent.com/pod-product-compliance
Lightning Source LLC
LaVergne TN
LVHW021353080426
835508LV00020B/2271

www.ingramcontent.com/pod-product-compliance
Lightning Source LLC
Chambersburg PA
CBHW071403090426
42737CB00011B/1335